PANDAS
Let's Meet Mrs. Huggs

The giant panda also known as panda bear or simply panda, is a bear. Giant pandas are on the brink of extinction, with just over 1,000 pandas left in the world. Scientists are hoping to increase the wild panda population to 5,000 by 2025.

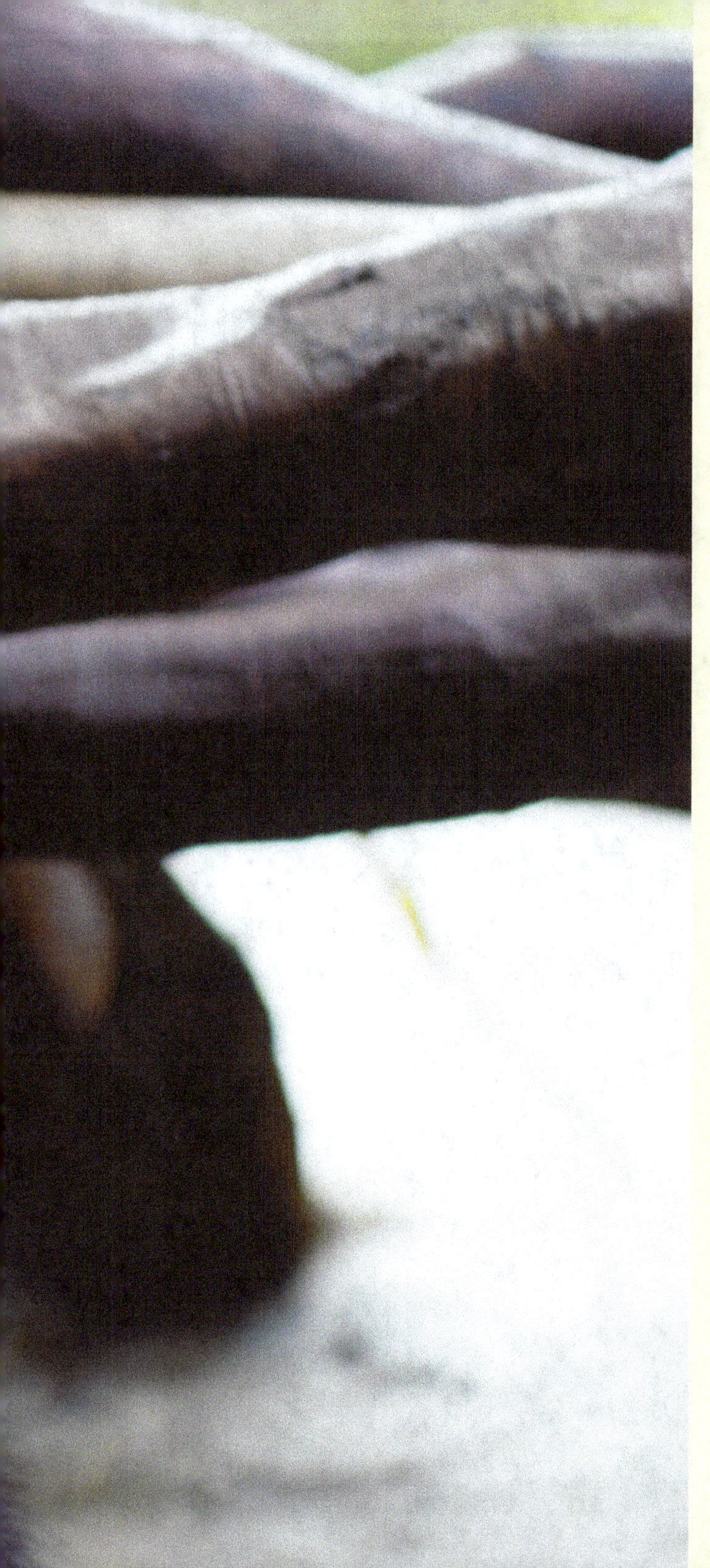

Giant pandas live in a few mountain ranges in central China, in Sichuan, Shaanxi, and Gansu provinces. They once lived in lowland areas, but farming, forest clearing, and other development now restrict giant pandas to the mountains.

The giant panda's diet is over 99% bamboo. It's stomach is ideal for digesting bamboo. The walls of the stomach are extra-muscular to digest the wood of the bamboo. The stomach is also covered inside with mucus that prevents it from being punctured by splinters.

Young pandas stay with the mothers for as long as three years, which means that a wild panda may raise only three or four cubs in a lifetime.

The giant panda
typically lives
around 20 years
in the wild and
up to 30 years
in captivity. The
oldest captive,
a female named
Ming Ming,
had a recorded
age of 34.

Pandas have
been a symbol of
peace in China.
For example,
hundreds of years
ago, warring
tribes in China
would raise a flag
with a picture
of a panda on it
to stop a battle
or call a truce.

A male Panda is
called a boar and
can weigh 175–
250 pounds and
Female Pandas
are called sows
and can weigh
150-230 pounds.

Giant pandas
are loners. They
dislike being
around other
pandas so much
that they have a
heightened sense
of smell that lets
them know when
another panda
is nearby so it
can be avoided.

The only time that these pandas seek each other out is during mating season. A panda's entire mating process takes only about two or three days. Males will use their smelling ability to find a female when they are ready to mate.

Giant pandas
will climb 13,000
feet (3,962 m) up
the mountains
of their home
area to feed on
higher slopes in
the summer.

A Panda's skin
is two different
colors. The skin
under their black
fur is dark while
the skin under the
white fur is pink!

It takes about
five years for
a female cub
to become an
adult and up to
seven years for
a male cub.

The eyespots of a giant panda cub are initially in the shape of a circle. As the cub grows, the circles become shaped like a teardrop.

Although a giant panda's fur looks silky and soft, it is quite thick and wiry. The hair of an adult giant panda can grow up to 4 inches long.

A giant panda's appetite for bamboo is insatiable. They eat bamboo 12 hours a day. The reason they eat so much is that bamboo is low in nutrients.